WHAT PEOPLE ARE SAYING ABOUT

WEB OF LIFE

Web of Life is a new way of looking at and working with ancient knowledge, which makes it immensely practical and useful for people now. Exploring the mysteries but also the great pragmatism of the medicine wheel in a number of different cultures Yvonne distils its essence and brings it alive, making it something you can create for yourself and work with to find answers to your personal questions and guidance for your life journey.
Ross Heaven, author, *Medicine for the Soul*, Founder of the Four Gates Foundation

Yvonne Ryves gives beautiful yet straightforward exercises in helping each one of us to find our place in her Web of Life. For example, with drum or rattle, the power of the directions is revealed not by what others say, but by what they say to you, she notes, giving brief synopses of various peoples' medicine wheel teachings. A slender but informative text, Web of Life provides clearly stated tools for understanding complex issues, along with practical steps to personal discovery such as creating personal Pathway Cards and Web Cards to aid in understanding one's past, present and future. I found it delightful!
Jim Pathfinder Ewing, author of *Reiki Shamanism: A Guide to Out-of-Body Healing*

For those living in contemporary society it is important to find our own way of making sense of our lives, our own connections to the world around us. Everything that exists is interconnected but how can you find your way to connect with it all, to hear the cation that contains messages for you.?
 In her book *Web of Life* Yvonne Ryves

exercises designed to give a sense of direction through creating something that belongs uniquely to you. These exercises take you through creating your own sacred space; finding and connecting with teachers relevant to you and creating physical cards and methods you can use to weave your own web.

Yvonne touches on the background and theories *Web of Life* is based on, including the medicine wheel, sacred hoop and web, and includes her own experiences as a useful comparison. However the real strength of this book is in the exercises, which are ideally suited for those who are looking for practical tools to start or develop their own practice and path through life.

June Kent, Editor *Indie Shaman Magazine*

Web of Life is a tribute to the dedication, inspiration and passion of Yvonne Ryves as a highly experienced Shamanic Practitioner and life coach. Her creative new approach to Medicine Wheel work makes this traditional indigenous tool for spiritual living much more accessible to contemporary travellers on the path of spiritual and intuitive living.

Dr. Mike Meredith, co-founder of UK Shamanism Today and Cambridge Healing & Holistic Lifestyle Group

Web of Life is very insightful, enjoyable and practical. The writing is concise and to the point, with the focus on the practical work, and creating the web of life for ourselves. The book is written in a great step-by-step format, so you can easily work through the book. I liked that after doing each exercise, there was further information on beliefs from different cultures and other inspirational ideas in case you needed some guidance. I enjoyed the creative aspect of making your own cards to use, finding it playful yet symbolic. Overall, I would highly recommend the book, it's beautifully written, thought provoking, and with gentle guidance directs you to discover the Web of Life for yourself.

Olive Kiely, Therapist, Reiki Master and Psychotherapy Student

This is a lovely practical, step-by-step guide on how to be the creator of your own web of life. Through following the outlined exercises in each chapter, the author engages you in an interactive process, gently guiding, empowering and encouraging you to take ownership, in being the creator of your own pathway. Thus developing a better understanding and clearer sense of being connected to your own journey through life. I particularly like the amount of useful and relevant background information that is given in each chapter, using examples of teachings from other cultures and belief systems and the continual encouragement, to use only what resonates with you. This book gives a brilliant framework and useful tools to guide you on your journey.

Jayne Bolster, Reg Nurse and Reiki Master/Practitioner

For years I felt a connection to all things natural and knew instinctively this is how we are meant to be, connected to our earth and all the creatures we share it with. But, I felt lost spiritually as I had no format to explain and share my unconventional feelings and beliefs. I was stuck on a path not knowing where to go or who to guide me and not understanding what belief system I belonged to. Until I read this book! Yvonne Ryves shares her own personal experiences and offers her simple tools to allow you to weave your own web. You can determine who your teachers are and to pinpoint what area of your life may require work, or indeed where next to explore on your path. Creating my own web of life has brought me to a place where I no longer feel Spiritually confined and now understand that there is no "One size fits all" formula. *Web of Life* helps you to focus on what feels right and what resonates on a personal level to reawaken that connection. *Web of Life* will allow us all to experience the world and our lives how we should .... Connected!

Lorraine Melia, Retail Training/Development and Resource Officer

Shaman Pathways
Web of Life

A new approach to using ancient
ways in these contemporary and
often challenging times to
weave your life path

Shaman Pathways
Web of Life

A new approach to using ancient
ways in these contemporary and
often challenging times to
weave your life path

Yvonne Ryves

MOON
BOOKS

Winchester, UK
Washington, USA

First published by Moon Books, 2013
Moon Books is an imprint of John Hunt Publishing Ltd., Laurel House, Station Approach,
Alresford, Hants, SO24 9JH, UK
office1@jhpbooks.net
www.johnhuntpublishing.com
www.moon-books.net

For distributor details and how to order please visit the 'Ordering' section on our website.

ISBN: 978 1 78099 960 9

A CIP catalogue record for this book is available from the British Library.

Design: Stuart Davies

Printed and bound by CPI Group (UK) Ltd, Croydon, CR0 4YY

We operate a distinctive and ethical publishing philosophy in all
areas of our business, from our global network of authors to
production and worldwide distribution.

CONTENTS

Dedication

To Martin, my husband and best friend, for his unwavering and unquestioning support. Thank you for never asking why.

Acknowledgements

There are many people who have contributed to Web of Life even though they may have been totally unaware of their contributions.

About six years ago I first met Maureen Murnan who then and over the following three years, introduced me not only to the Native American Medicine Wheel but also the idea that within the Medicine Wheel were teachers whom Native American cultures e.g. Lakota, would work with in ceremony and in their daily lives and which we too could use to help ourselves. Having sown the seeds these ideas kept working away in my subconscious finally blossoming into what is now the Web of Life.

Along side this Jacqueline Bourbon and John Brett who I met at the same time as I met Maureen, were very instrumental early on in my shamanic work and from them I began to learn to listen to trees, plants, birds, and more besides.

More recently I am indebted to Jayne Bolster, Olive Kiely and Lorraine Melia, my test readers for Web of Life, and June Kent who proof read and edited an early version. Thank you all for giving so willingly of your very valuable time. I really appreciate the help that you all gave me through your wise and always practical feedback.

I would also like to thank Margaret Garrow who made the beautiful spiders' web with shaman's crystal spider that hangs over my treatment room door, a constant reminder that I too have webs to weave.

This book would have been much less without all of you

Introduction

We are what we create.
Nothing exists until we create it.
Yvonne Ryves

The web of life is a complex structure and we travel without a map or GPS system to help us navigate our path through it. Many of us move through our lives unsure of how we fit in or where we are. We buy self-help books by the score often to be dissatisfied and no nearer finding whatever it is we seek; the truth of who we are, what we are, or of where we fit in. We search for teachers and often find ourselves following the path of others because they seem, for a time at least, to have the answers. We spend our lives seeking a way to access the knowledge that is within us and the truth that surrounds us.

Without a framework of some kind to guide and support us we may suffer a loss of connection to our spiritual self, whereas with one, we can develop a sense of direction and a conscious connection to who and where we are.

The idea of a wheel, sacred hoop, or web is found in many cultures or belief systems such as Native American, Peruvian, Celtic, Wicca, Siberian and Buddhist to name but a few. People who are born into such a life often have a strong base to guide and support them. It is no accident or coincidence that there is such a resurgence of interest in working with medicine wheels at this time for this represents a growing need within society for some form of guidance and structure.

Every single one of us lives our lives within a wheel, a circle, a hoop or a web and every single one of us can benefit from learning how to live our lives to the full within it. The problem though, for many of us, is that because we do not belong to the culture of a medicine wheel or wheel of direction, we find that the wheels do not really fit us or we have trouble connecting with or remembering the attributes.

This is actually quite a problem, as not only do we not belong to the culture in question, many of us do not even belong to any single culture. We are in fact, the product of a mix of cultures, of intercultural marriages over time and of an increasingly mobile world. This will continue for globalization of cultures is as prevalent as globalization of businesses.

The internet gives us access to the teachings of other cultures and belief systems and within us we feel a stirring of recognition when we touch those that resonate with our past, our current blood line, or even our past lives, for more and more we are remembering who we are and where we have come from. This can leave us feeling lost and confused, or maybe even feeling as if we belong somewhere else. This is why it is important for us to develop our own way of making sense of our lives, one that takes into account the myriad of cultures that feel right for us or are part of us.

I was first introduced to the medicine wheel several years ago when attending a course on Native American Spiritualism and Culture. I loved the idea of being able to work in the wheel, for it to guide my path and help me learn but despite having the opportunity to deepen my knowledge and understanding over the intervening years, I continued to struggle with it and do to this day.

I struggled with the meaning and teachers assigned to the directions, with holding on to what they are and with trying to find a way of remembering them as much as I wanted to. In other words I struggled with finding a meaningful way to use the medicine wheel in my life.

Even the discovery that different Native American tribes had different teachers connected to the directions did not really help me other than to bring the realization that there was no one size fits all.

Then I discovered the Andean medicine wheel with different attributes and a different way of working. I then began to realize that I actually needed some aspects of the Andean wheel and some of the Lakota wheel for me even to begin to feel at home but even then something was not right.

Gradually as time passed and my learning progressed I began to understand that it is not about adjusting anyone else's wheel to meet your needs, it is about creating something that is uniquely yours, something that belongs to you and which serves to help you know where you are, who you are working with and which will help you remember that it is you who are bringing everything into being, you who are the creator.

This is where the web of life comes in for it is a map, a guide, a teacher and with it we are never truly lost.

What follows is both my interpretation of weaving a web of life and at times, a record of my understanding of the process. It is there to help others take on the ultimate role of creator, both of the tools they can work with and of their path through the web of life. It may have begun with the medicine wheel but how it ends up depends on you.

Throughout the book you will find exercises that are designed to help you create your own web of life. They should be carried out in the order they are given in the book as they are sequential and build upon one another. There is no time limit on completing each of the exercises; some will be quickly finished whereas others will take longer depending on your own life experiences and knowledge.

Chapter One

The Web Of Life: the interconnectedness of all things

I see the solution in each problem as being detectable in the pattern and web of the whole. The connections between causes and effects are often more subtle and complex than our rough and ready understanding of the physical world might naturally suppose 1. Adams D (1988) Dirk Gently's Holistic Detective Agency

In general we have a very limited view of the world around us and so are only aware of a fraction of what exists, what we have access to, what we impact on and what impacts on us. Due to this we are really only scratching the surface of what is around us and what we can use to help and support us in our lives, if only we knew how to connect with it all.

The late science fiction writer Douglas Adams used his awareness of the fundamental interconnectedness of all things to help his fictional 'holistic detective' to solve cases, if we also develop our awareness and understanding of the connections that exist we too can use them to help us find answers to where we are, what is happening and where we are going.

So what is this 'web of life', this 'interconnectedness of all things'?

Many cultures and belief systems, both scientific and esoteric, have an understanding of threads and connections that connect not only human to human but to every living thing. Although they may come from differing viewpoints and with varying explanations there is a general consensus that these threads or connections and the communication between everything that exists is real and that all life forms on the planet communicate and interact in some way.

4

In Buddhism, enlightenment is seen as an awakening to the true nature of life, which includes the realization that all things are interconnected. Buddhists believe that there is an inseparable relationship between the individual and the environment.

In Shamanism it is also believed that we are not separate from nature but a part of it.

Shamanism teaches us that everything that exists is alive and has a spirit. Shamans speak of a web of life that connects all of life and the spirit that lives in all things. Everything on earth is interconnected and any belief that we are separate from other life forms including the earth, stars, wind, etc is purely an illusion. 2. Ingerman S (2011) Shamanism: Healing of Individuals and the Planet (abstract on shamanism)

Dennis Meehan, Eagle Soaring, lecturer and Medicine Wheel Artist, is one of many individuals around the world who works with humans to help them develop an understanding that there is no separation between mankind, the animal kingdom, the plants and rocks.

All things on Earth have a common bond. When Earth Mother speaks to you, or the animals come to you, this is a message from the Great Spirit. Learn this simple wisdom and you can break down barriers that keep you stuck. 3. Eagle Soaring, The Interconnectedness of All Things Taught through Medicine Wheel Art

Wiccans also believe that everything that exists is connected and is part of a circle of vibrating energy like a spider's web or electronic grid and that this can be spoken of as the web of life or nature's web.

Pagans have in fact, always held the beliefs that everything is connected and shares consciousness, that humans are a part of this consciousness not above it or separate from it, and that all parts of the web of life are equal in value.

In terms of science, Quantum Physics when speaking about the subatomic particles that make up all forms of life can only describe them in terms of how they interconnect and act with one another. In String Theory these particles are described as containing vibrating, dancing strings with each sending out different vibrations or notes. This therefore can be seen as supporting the view that all life is interconnected and communicates, even at subatomic level.

Robert Lanza and Bob Berman writing about Biocentrism speak about humans being at the:

heart of a great web of space and time whose threads are connected according to laws that dwell in our minds 4. Lanza R with Berman B (April 2009) Biocentrism: How Life and Consciousness Are the Keys to Understanding the True Nature of the Universe:

In their article 'The Web of Life', writing in relation to how connected we are, Harry Massey and David R Hamilton PH.D encourage us to;

Think of a spider's web. Now imagine that every person on the planet is a node on that web, with its strands connecting them. Then imagine that this web is so big that it connects not just all of us, but everything in the universe. If such a thing existed, then every choice that each of us made would create vibrations - ripples or waves- on the web that would be felt everywhere and by everyone. In this way we would be in constant communication with the whole universe exchanging information and energy through the vibrations we create, and also those that we feel. Each choice we made would be information that would ripple outward, interacting with the rest of the web. 5. Hamilton D.R and Massey H (5 April

2012) The Web of Life, excerpted from Choice Point: Align Your Purpose:

They also cite Professor of Quantum Information Theory at Oxford University, Vlatko Vedral who believes that we constantly exchange information with the universe as a whole and that because of this, it is impossible to think of ourselves as separate from either our surroundings or each other.

Vedral also states that:

The point is, we are intimately connected in a deeper and much more fundamental way than we ever imagined, and that as we exchange information with reality, it's as if we 'speak' with it. 6. Hamilton D.R and Massey H (5 April 2012) The Web of Life, excerpted from Choice Point: Align Your Purpose

Ecopsychology, the science of healing, counseling and healing with nature encourages us to recognize that we are part of the web of life and so part of the balance of life. Only by being aware of the connections we have with everything can we find balance in our own lives.

One way of finding this balance is to learn not only to speak with reality, but to listen to it and learn from it. In this way you may also learn to move through your life both with a clearer understanding of the interconnectedness of everything and of how you can harness some of these connections to help and support you.

If you think about the myriad of connections that exist within the web of life and the fact that through these connections we may obtain information, knowledge, support, help and guidance, you may start to see how disconnected and isolated humans have become.

Everything that exists can communicate with us in some way as explained in the vibrations or notes of String Theory. If we then follow the belief that in this communication there are messages for us then it may follow that all we need to do is to learn how to listen to and utilize these connections.

To do this it is important to find ways to reconnect with the world around us and the connections within it, not through books, the Internet or television but through experiential inter-action.

Chapter Two

Weaving Your Own Web of Life

The concept that we are in constant communication with everything that exists can be both an exciting and yet daunting one. It is possible to imagine that as we open up and become aware of connections we may become bombarded with information, that it might be like being in a crowded room where everyone is trying to speak to us at the same time; sheer chaos and completely overwhelming. But it does not need to be like this.

Once we can be open to the idea that it is both possible and useful, to utilize the lines of communication that are available to us we can learn how to do this in a way that is manageable and beneficial, rather than overwhelming for us.

One way of doing this is to think of yourself as the creator of your own section of the web of life and through this to learn how to open up the connections that will help you the most. All this means is deciding who and what, out of all the things that exist, you wish to communicate with. By working through the exercises in the web of life you will in fact learn to do just this.

If we take Massey and Hamilton's analogy of the spider's web and use this as a symbol for the web of life, we can also use the spider as a symbol for each and every one of us, working away, spinning our own section of the web.

By envisaging yourself as the spider in the center of the web, it may also then be possible for you to imagine yourself creating your own web. By weaving into your web as you spin, the connections that are useful for you, all the time maintaining control over what these connections are and how many of them you are open to, you can create something that is uniquely yours.

In fact, the more you are able to see yourself at the center of your part of the web of life and so as creator of your web, the more you will be able to learn to connect with your own inner wisdom in terms of the connections that you make, for just as the spider is responsible for creating its own web, so you are responsible for creating your own reality.

Those working with a Medicine Wheel would speak about the connections you create within your own reality, as being teachers i.e. connections that we can learn from and which can support us and help us heal and grow as we move through our lives.

The symbolism of the spider's web as representing the web of life is an important one for the web is seen as a symbol of industry, patience and flexibility. It may look like a fragile, magical space but it also has great strength, with its construction based on sacred geometry, the geometry of creation. The shapes and paths within it form a secure framework with connections from one path to another, thus serving as a reminder of the interconnectedness of all things within the web of life.

As you weave your web of life, weaving in the connections or teachers that you are drawn to working with, you will also be creating paths within it. As you learn to work within your own web it will become possible for you to know not only where in the web you are, but also where you are going and which path you are choosing to take. Likewise you will also learn how to communicate with the connections or teachers that you have woven into your web.

Early on in the development of this work I was sat with the outline of a medicine wheel in front of me. Suddenly I saw that in the center of this wheel was a spider and the legs of the spider formed the spokes of the wheel giving me eight compass directions. For me this was a moment of complete revelation. Once I had seen that the spider was at the heart of my wheel, I ceased to see the wheel but instead saw the web and the possibility of all the pathways I could weave. The medicine wheel had become a web of life, with me, the spider and weaver, at the center of my own creation.

Spider teaches us that we are the center of our own world and that if we know ourselves, we will know the universe. Part of spider's wisdom is in connection with the web of life and the interconnectedness of all. It teaches us that it is ourselves who create our lives and destiny, as well as how to face reality. Spider also teaches that everything we do now, is weaving what we will encounter in the future and that the past always influences both the present and the future. This reinforces further, the need for us to be able to see and know where we are, what has gone before and what we are weaving into the path we are creating ahead of us. In other words how we are weaving our own web of life.

The glittering web sits silently over my door
The spider hidden in the gossamer threads
Spins quietly and diligently
Without me noticing
Drawing me into the darkness
And by doing so
Into the light
Yvonne Ryves

Chapter Three

Circles and Cycles

Before you begin to create your own web in which to work it is helpful to get a sense of what others use or have used before. This is not so you may 'copy' but because for each person reading this there is likely to be something that catches their attention, feels right, resonates or sits well with them.

Mankind has always been drawn to circles and wheels, for our lives and those of other living things follow cycles, for example:

- birth, death and rebirth
- the phases we pass through as we move through life
- the phases of the moon that affect the tides and can also affect us
- the cycles of hibernation or dormancy experienced by some animals and plants
- the water cycle, which brings and takes away life

We have cycles of change, developmental cycles, seasonal cycles and many more besides.

The medicine wheel is an eclectic version of a cycle, the directions nominally associated with seasons but a cycle that can occur at any time during the year.

But before the wheel, came the circle so that is where we will start.

Stone circles were possibly created so that the annual movement of the sun could be followed. Pre-Christians built labyrinths to help them understand both the path of life and their spiritual path. For Hindus the wheel of existence is represented within a circle and in China Yin and Yang are within a universal circle. Tibetan Llamas create sacred universe within a circle of sand painting and the sacred circle is part of Native American artwork, healing practice and rituals.

The circle is also the basis for many homes, the yurt, the tepee, the hooghan, the ger and of course tents.

Circles are one of the building blocks of the universe and a form in sacred geometry. Wherever we look in nature we can see examples of circles, in the shell of a snail, the petals of some flowers, the eyes of animals and humans, and of course in the web of a spider.

A circle is also a shape that many of us find pleasing to the eye. We surround ourselves with them in our lives: flower and plant pots, cups, mugs glasses and plates, lights, cushions, mirrors and the wheels on bikes, cars or prams for example. They are the shape of drums, mandalas and of crop circles and we ascribe many attributes to them, for example: wholeness, unity, perfection, purity, infinity and completion

There is also much symbolism attached to circles. A circle could be said to represent the sun or moon, the sacred or the divine, to represent the infinite nature of energy or even the inclusiveness of the universe. Some say a circle symbolizes the whole, all possibilities, everything that has been, is and is yet to come.

Others may see the circle as representing sacred space, the line forming a boundary allowing us to contain the power we create within it, holding it there until we are ready to release it. Seen in this way the circle represents a reflection of itself above and below the plane in which we physically work.

A circle can mark out and set aside space for those who travel between worlds e.g. in shamanic journeying. In Wicca the circle is described as a doorway through which threads can be drawn from the world of spirit and woven into new patterns. The circle can therefore create a symbolic doorway for us to reach through and touch other realities so that we may bring back insight and wisdom. It is part of the world of spirit and a place of connection.

Chapter Four

Creating Sacred Space

Knowledge of how to create sacred space is very important for anyone weaving their web of life. As you weave your web and in time weave in the teachers that you choose to work with, it is good to be able to connect with them and learn what they have to offer. Connecting with them in sacred space means that you do so in a space that is clear and with a conscious intention. A circle is often used to create sacred space and you may feel drawn to use one too.

The ideal sacred space is one that you carry inside you. It is the quiet space, the inner aloneness even within a crowd, a sacred inner space you carry within your mind, a sacred space that is part of you.

This will develop over time and to help this happen it is useful to practice creating sacred space in a physical way, for it is this which can help you to feel safe and give you the freedom to connect with your teachers.

There are many ways of creating sacred space. Some people like to have a special place in which to work. This may be a room, a place in the garden, a blanket spread on the ground or even a chair they like to sit in.

Exercise I
- Have a good look around you and find a space that feels as if it is somewhere you would like to work.
- Once you have decided where you would like to work you need to find a way to create sacred space.
- The suggestions that follow are ways that you might want to try out to find what suits you, or you may already have a way of your own.

Setting an intention

Many of the ways of creating sacred space talk of setting an intention. This is just the same as holding a thought or idea and trusting that it will happen.

You could say something like:

I intend that the space that I am in is sacred space. That I may work in it safely and that I am protected here.

Smudging

Sage, sweet grass or other herbs can be used to smudge and cleanse space for you to work in. Bundles of these can be purchased from health shops, new age shops or online or you can dry your own herbs to make into bundles to use. An inflammable container to catch any sparks and a large feather to brush smoke around are also useful.

- Hold the intention, or thought, to cleanse the area or room you have chosen and to create sacred space in which to work.
- Light the herb bundle and blow on it gently until you have plenty of smoke.
- Being careful not to set fire to anything, you can start by cleansing yourself. You do this by wafting smoke over and around you either with your hand or the feather.
- Then use the bundle to wave smoke around the area or room paying attention to any corners. Let the smoke billow into these. You can use the feather to help the smoke go where you would like it to go.
- Make sure you have extinguished the herb bundle when you have finished.
- You can now work in the sacred space you have created.

Opening/Casting and closing a circle

There is no one way to open or close a circle and if you work with Wicca you will have your own way. This though is a very simple way to open a circle to create sacred space to work in and to close it when you have finished.

Opening/Casting

- Choose a place to cast your circle.
- Decide if you are going to draw it by visualizing (imagining) it in the air, or physically drawing it on the ground with chalk.
- Circles are usually aligned to the four cardinal directions of East, South, West and North so use a compass to work out where these are.
- You will need five candles or markers, one for each direction and one for the center.
- Place these on the ground in each direction and the center.
- Hold the intention, or thought to create sacred space in which to work.
- If you are drawing the circle on the ground then start in the East and moving clockwise, enclosing each of your candles and markers, draw your circle in chalk.
- If you are drawing the circle in the air then with you arm held out straight, start in the East and visualize or imagine your arm drawing a circle enclosing your candles or markers.
- You can then work inside the circle in the sacred space you have created.

Closing

It is very important to close the circle when you have finished working.

Start in the East this time moving anticlockwise, rub out or visualize your circle being removed.

Call the directions and ask for their help and support

There are many chants or poems that you can use to call in the directions. This though is a very simple way.

- Before you start you will need to use a compass to find each of the four cardinal directions – North, East, South and West.
- Mark the rest of the directions with a marker or a candle.
- Hold the intention, or thought, to create sacred space in which to work.
- Stand in the center of the circle.
- Face East and ask the energies and/or spirits of the East to be with you and help create sacred space.
- Turn to the South and ask the energies and/or spirits of the South to be with you and help create sacred space.
- Turn to the West and ask the energies and/or spirits of the West to be with you and help create sacred space.
- Turn to the North and ask the energies and/or spirits of the North to be with you and help create sacred space.
- You can now work inside the sacred space you have created.

Call your ancestors, guides or helpers and ask them to be with you and help you.

- Choose the space in which you are going to work.
- Sit quietly and focus on your breath, this helps to calm and center you.
- When you feel nice and calm invite your ancestors, guides or helpers to be with you, to protect you and keep you safe while you are working.
- You can then work in the sacred space you have created.

Drum or rattle

If you have a drum or rattle you can work with it to clear and create sacred space and raise the vibration of the space you have chosen to work in.

- Hold the intention or thought to create sacred space.
- Hold the drum or rattle in your hand and start to play.
- Let the drum or rattle find the rhythm or beat that it needs, you will probably find this changes as you move around.
- Move around the space or room paying attention to any corners.
- You may even like to create a circle around you with your drum or rattle.
- Continue until you feel the drumming or rattling is finished.
- You can then work in the sacred space you have created.

Cocoon yourself in white or pale blue light

- Choose the space in which you are going to work.
- Sit quietly and focus on your breath, this helps to calm and center you.
- When you feel nice and calm imagine yourself surrounded by a bubble of white or pale blue light.
- Imagine the light above you, below you and on all four sides of you.
- See yourself moving around inside the bubble.
- Know that inside your bubble is sacred space and that you are safe to work here.

Use Reiki power symbols and intention

If you have Reiki you use the power symbols to create sacred space.

- Choose the space you would like to work in.
- Stand in the center of the space.

- Hold the intention to create sacred space.
- Draw a large power symbol over the area and step into it.
- Draw four more power symbols, one on each side of you, as well as in front and behind you. They can be close to you or further away whatever feels right.
- This creates the sacred space for you to work in.

Create a crystal pyramid

- Choose the space in which you are going to work.
- Sit quietly in the center of the space and focus on your breath.
- Hold the intention to create sacred space.
- Wait until you feel calm and then visualize or imagine a crystal pyramid forming around you.
- The pyramid has a four-sided base and four sides, one on each side of you going up to a point above you.
- You can make the pyramid as large as you wish.
- You can make the pyramid from whatever crystal you wish e.g. Rose Quartz, Amethyst or Clear Quartz.
- Feel the strength of the pyramid around you.
- You have now created sacred space in which to work.

It is important that you do whatever you need to feel that you are in a sacred, protected space in which you feel safe. Experiment and change what you do until it feels right for you. There is no right way of doing this, only what feels right for you.

When working in sacred space it is also important to be grounded. If you do not know how to ground yourself then experiment with the following steps, which are simple grounding exercises and see what works for you.

You may already have your own grounding exercises but you might still like to try those in Exercises 2-4 or alternatively go straight on to Chapter Five.

Exercise 2

- Go outside and find a quiet space with some grass, where you will be undisturbed.
- Take your shoes off and walk barefoot on the grass.
- With every step be aware of your foot and its connection with the grass and the Earth.
- As you walk, breathe in deeply as you place each foot on the Earth.
- Focus only on your breathing, the feel of the grass and the Earth energy as it flows into you.

Exercise 3

- Sit quietly with your feet flat on the floor, without shoes is best, and make sure your spine is straight.
- Close your eyes and imagine, sense or visualize roots flowing from the soles of your feet into the Earth (Do not worry if you are not on the ground floor this will still work).
- Send the roots flowing down, spreading out beneath your feet and anchoring firmly into the Earth.
- Now breathe in deeply imagining the breath coming up from the Earth into the soles of your feet, up your legs and into your body.
- Continue this for a few minutes at least and with every breath feel the connection between the soles of your feet and the Earth becoming stronger as if a magnet is pulling you.

Exercise 4

- Sit quietly with your feet flat on the floor, without shoes is best, and make sure your spine is straight.
- Close your eyes and imagine, sense or visualize a Lotus Flower opened out beneath you and yourself sat upon it.
- Imagine, visualize, sense or simply know that the roots of

the Lotus Flower flow deep into the Earth beneath you.

- Now breathe in deeply imagining the breath coming up from the Earth into the base of your spine and into your body.
- Continue this for a for as long as you wish and with every breath feel the Earth energy flowing up into your body, breathing the energy up into you as far as feels comfortable for you.

Drumming

Drumming is the sound closest to our own heartbeat and in itself can be very grounding so if you drum then try using the drum to ground you within sacred space.

Now that you have learnt how to create your own sacred space and how to ground yourself within it, it is time to learn about Compass Pathways.

Chapter Five

The Compass Pathways

If you are to know where you have been, where you are and where you are going then it is useful to have something to help you see both your position and your path. Although you are not actually working with a medicine wheel, the structure of the wheel is important, for it will hold the web that you are to weave. The compass pathways provide paths and connections so you may move easily around your web.

By weaving your web in this way, a web within a wheel, you will be working with a balance of energies. The web being woven by you represents creative energy and indeed you as the spider, the wheel holding you so that you do not get carried away, go off course or get lost, represents a more logical, controlling energy.

We are all moving into a time when we need to find a way to be in balance both in ourselves and with all that is around us. By merging the creative and logical energies in this way with both energies playing their part, both doing what they do best but neither dominant, you can help to bring that balance into your life.

It is not necessary though for you to understand medicine wheels, sacred hoops or other cultural wheels in order to work with the compass directions or pathways, or to weave your own web of life but nevertheless it is interesting to see how different cultures have adapted wheels to suit their own culture and beliefs. This may also give you ideas as to the teachers you may weave into your own web, but first there is work to be done.

Exercise 5

From now on you will need to have a notebook to hand as you

read and move through the exercises.

Throughout the book you will find numbered exercises, which you will need to complete in the order they are presented. It is these exercises that will teach you and guide you, as you become the creator weaving your web of life and creating the tools that you will be able to work with. Be prepared for this work to take time and not to rush. Leave ideas time to gel or develop and also for your ideas to change. There will be further exercises later to build on what you do here and to help develop your own teachers within your web of life. Not everything has to be done at once.

Before you move on, take a few minutes to write down any ideas or thoughts that you have had so far about your own web of life.

Cardinal Pathways

The North
Exercise 6

- Make sure you have your notebook and something to write with.
- Find a quiet place to sit; somewhere you will not be disturbed.
- Brainstorm or create a mind map of all your ideas of what the North represents **to you.**
- Record everything that comes to you.
- You might like to think of any feelings, emotions, colors, animals, behaviors, attitudes and so on that you connect with the North.
- Complete this task before moving on but be prepared to return to your notes as new thoughts come to you concerning the North.

As we begin to look at some of the qualities, teachers and

attributes that other cultures connect to the North it may trigger new ideas for you. It is important that these new ideas really resonate with you and that you are not focusing on them simply to fill your notebook. The information given in Exercises 6 - 15, about the attributes that various cultures give to the directions, is a complete simplification of these attributes; it is in no way exhaustive and is not designed to teach you about the various cultures in any way. The intention is to help you to develop your own ideas of the compass pathways and their meaning for you

Exercise 7
- Before you start reading find your notebook.
- If something you read catches your attention make a note of it.
- Why you have done so may not make sense now but may when you work later.
- Nothing you are drawn to record will be wasted.

Cree
Cree teachings are based on a circular pattern with four seasons, four stages of life, four aspects of self. The Cree see the North as a place of achievement, reflection, deep connections, spirituality and understanding of life. White in the North is for the White Nation and for Buffalo Woman. The North is also a place of knowledge, wisdom, freedom, selfishness, person power, eldership, the element Fire and of winter.

Cherokee
The Cherokee work with seven sacred directions and their medicine wheel consists of four green logs extending outwards from the Sacred Fire, whilst recognizing the directions of Above, Within and Below. The North for the Cherokee connects to blue, the element of Air, the season of winter and the time of midnight. It represents defeat, surrender and trouble.

Inca

For the Inca the wheel has four directions. The element of the North is Air. The North represents wisdom, knowledge the mind and animals. The Hummingbird is found here, as are the ancestors or ancient ones. The enemy in the North is clarity and the task here is to stop the world.

Celtic

The Celtic wheel is divided into eight sections or stations. In the Celtic wheel the North represents darkness, midnight, the Earth, mountains, landscape, stones and minerals. The Earth Goddess and Horned God belong in the North, as does the silver wheel of Arianhrod representing the silver wheel of stars. It is a place of ice, of frozen potential, of waiting to be born and the time is Yule or Winter Solstice on 21st December, a festival of joy and light. This is the time of the Triple Goddess and the birth of the Sun God.

Mayan

In the North, the Mayan place the element of Air, the color white, animal, people and the human mind.

Tibetan

In the Tibetan wheel the sword, family, water and green belong in the North.

Siberian

In Siberia the North is the direction of 'behind' and holds violent weather, lightning and tornados.

Exercise 8

- By now you may have begun to agree and disagree with the connections made between others and the North. This is as it should be.

- Be discerning.
- Review what you have in your notes and use what is there to write a full description of what you consider the North to be and why.
- Do not worry if this feels incomplete or imperfect. You will have the rest of your life to change your mind, adjust your ideas and amend your beliefs.

The East
Exercise 9

- When you feel you have finished with the North, for now at least, find your notebook and begin to work with the East.
- Find a quiet place to sit; somewhere you will not be disturbed.
- Brainstorm or create a mind map of all your ideas of what the East represents **to you**. Record everything that comes to you.
- You might like to think of any feelings, emotions, colors, animals, behaviors, attitudes and so on that you connect with the East.
- Complete this task before moving on but be prepared to return to your notes as new thoughts come to you concerning the East.
- If anything you read from now on catches your attention make a note of it. Why you have done so may not make sense now but may when you work later.
- Nothing you are drawn to record will be wasted.

Cree

The Cree see the East as the beginning of new things for the sun rises in the East and it is a new day. It is the direction of the Eagle, of focus, of yellow for the yellow nation and of the element of Air. East is the time of planting and of birth. It is a time of connecting to the physical.

Cherokee
The Cherokee perceive the East as being spring and the time as morning. It is the place of the color red and the element of Fire. The East represents victory, success, war, life and spirit.

Inca
In the Inca wheel East represents a time of meditation, praying and listening. It is a place to seek vision and purpose. The element of the East is Fire and the animal here is Condor.

Celtic
In the Celtic wheel the East is a place of ideas, new concepts, rebirth and illumination. A time of fertility and the festival of Ostata or Spring Equinox on 21st March, the first true day of spring. The Goddess is here as the Maiden and the God grows to maturity for the hours of dark and light are equal

Mayan
In the East, the Mayan place the element of Fire, the color yellow, human people and the human spirit.

Tibetan
In the Tibetan wheel vajra family, the color blue-black and the element of Air belong in the East.

Siberian
In Siberia the East is the direction of 'left', of femaleness and the sky spirits of disease and discord. It is also the place of Eagle and of non-edible animals.

Exercise 10
- As with the North you may now be agreeing and

disagreeing with the connections made between others and the East. Again this is as it should be.

- Be discerning.
- Review what you have in your notes and use what is there to write a full description of what you consider the East to be and why.
- Do not worry if this feels incomplete or imperfect. You will have the rest of your life to change your mind, adjust your ideas and amend your beliefs.

The South
Exercise 11

- When you feel you have finished with the East, for now at least, find your notebook and begin to work with the South.
- Find a quiet place to sit; somewhere you will not be disturbed.
- Brainstorm or create a mind map of all your ideas of what the South represents **to you.** Record everything that comes to you.
- You might like to think of any feelings, emotions, colors, animals, behaviors, attitudes and so on that you connect with the South.
- Complete this task before moving on but be prepared to return to your notes as new thoughts come to you concerning the South.
- If anything you read from now on catches your attention make a note of it. Why you have done so may not make sense now but may when you work later.
- Nothing you are drawn to record will be wasted.

Cree

South is red for the Red Nation, a direction of hard work, integrity, honesty and truth. Earth and mouse are found here. It is the season of summer, time of growth, adolescence and the development of mental capabilities.

Cherokee

The Cherokee see the South as representing harmony, healing and natural space. It is the direction of white, summer, the time of midday and of the element Earth.

Inca

Incas perceive South as the place of the serpent, of plants and emotions. Here we learn to release our past. For Inca the element of the South is Water.

Celtic

In the Celtic wheel the element of Fire is found in the South. Here the energy of the sun is strongest. It is a place of play and expansion and the festival is that of Litha or Summer Solstice on 21st June where Goddess and God are both mature and revel in the fertility of the Earth.

Mayan

In the South is the element of Water, the colors red and green, plants and emotions.

Tibetan

In the Tibetan wheel the jewel family, the color yellow and the element of Earth are connected with the South.

Siberian

In Siberia the South is the direction of 'front' and of Water Spirits.

Exercise 12

- Once again you may find yourself agreeing and

disagreeing with the connections made between others and the South. Again this is as it should be.

- Be discerning.
- Review what you have in your notes and use what is there to write a full description of what you consider the South to be and why.
- Do not worry if this feels incomplete or imperfect. You will have the rest of your life to change your mind, adjust your ideas and amend your beliefs.

The West
Exercise 13

- When you feel you have finished with the South, for now at least, find your notebook and begin to work with the West.
- Find a quiet place to sit; somewhere you will not be disturbed.
- Brainstorm or create a mind map of all your ideas of what the West represents **to you**. Record everything that comes to you.
- You might like to think of any feelings, emotions, colors, animals, behaviors, attitudes and so on that you connect with the West.
- Complete this task before moving on but be prepared to return to your notes as new thoughts come to you concerning the West.
- If anything you read from now on catches your attention make a note of it. Why you have done so may not make sense now but may when you work later.
- Nothing you are drawn to record will be wasted.

Cree

For the Cree the West is the direction of introspection and reflection, a place to go deep within and to heal. Bear and the element of Water are found here. The color is black for the Black Nation. It is the time of the harvest of adulthood and of deep understanding.

Cherokee

The Cherokee see the West as the season of autumn or fall, the time is evening, the color black and the element here is Water. The West represents death, change, impermanence and the ancestors.

Inca

For the Inca, West is introspection and intuition, of looking deeply within and is about daring to live fearlessly by stepping beyond the fear of death. The Jaguar is found here.

Celtic

In the Celtic wheel the festival of the West is Mabon or Autumn Equinox on 21st September. This is the second harvest and a time for rest. The West is the time of sunset and dusk, day and night once again being equal. This is a place of abundance. The color is green and it is seen as the gateway to the realms beyond physical life.

Mayan

In the Mayan Wheel of Directions the West represents the element of Earth, the stone people, the human body and the color black.

Tibetan

In the Tibetan wheel the lotus family, the color red and the element of Fire are connected with the West.

Siberian

In Siberia the West is the direction of 'right', of maleness, animals that provide food and is the home of benevolent sky spirits.

Exercise 14

- As before you have very likely found yourself agreeing and disagreeing with the connections made between others and the West. By now you will know that this is as it should be.
- Be discerning.
- Review what you have in your notes and use what is there to write a full description of what you consider the West to be and why.
- Do not worry if this feels incomplete or imperfect. You will have the rest of your life to change your mind, adjust your ideas and amend your beliefs.

'Cross Quarter' Pathways

One of the few cultures to include the 'cross quarter' directions of North East, South East, South West and North West on their wheels of direction are the Celts, whose wheel also forms the base for the Western traditions of wheels of directions such as Wicca.

These directions form an integral part of the web of life so it is important now to take the time to look as what is included in the views of others and to form your own understanding of what these directions mean for you. The only culture we are looking at here is Celtic.

Exercise 15

- Find a quiet place to sit; somewhere you will not be disturbed.
- Taking one cross quarter direction at a time create a mind map of all your ideas of what each of the cross quarter directions represents **to you.**

- Record everything that comes to you.
- You might like to think of any feelings, emotions, colors, animals, behaviors, attitudes and so on that you connect with each cross quarter direction.
- Complete this task before moving on but be prepared to return to your notes as new thoughts come to you concerning each of them.
- If anything you read from now on catches your attention make a note of it. Why you have done so may not make sense now but may when you work later.
- Nothing you are drawn to record will be wasted.

North East

The festival aligned with the North East is that of Imbolc on 1st February. This is the beginning of the Maiden aspect of Goddess and the Sun God seen as a young boy. The North East connects to the design of energy, the balance of male and female and the sacred marriage.

South East

The festival of the South East is Beltane on 1st May. This is a celebration of the renewal of life, a time of fertility, joy and passion, the Goddess as Maiden is fully fertile and the God fully grown to manhood. This direction connects to the ancestors of land and place as well as to personal ancestral memory.

South West

Lughnassadh or Lammas on 1st August is the festival of the South West and the time of the first harvest and thanksgiving. This is the Mother aspect of Goddess and a time of waning strength for the God This is the place of the dream weave where the future is being woven. It is the access point to the Web of Wyrd, the tapestry of life.

North West

The festival of Samhain on 1st November aligns with the North West. This is the time of the final harvest, a time to reflect, on what we have achieved (or not) and on what we are unable to control. A time for honoring the memory of our ancestors this is the time when the veil between worlds is at its thinnest. Thus we find here karma and lessons waiting to be learned along with patterns of illusion and projections of hope and fears.

Exercise 16

- Taking each of the cross quarter directions in turn reflect on your notes on each direction and decide which feel right for you.
- Write your own description of the North East, South East, South West and North West using your notes and adding your own thoughts, ideas, feelings and emotions to give a full picture.
- As always do not worry if this feels incomplete or imperfect. You will have the rest of your life to change your mind, adjust your ideas and amend your beliefs.

The work that you have done in creating a picture of your own beliefs and ideas about each direction and therefore each pathway will help form the basis of your work as creator in weaving your own web of life. Keep these notes safe for you will need them.

Chapter Six

Finding Your Connections or Teachers

Please make sure you have completed all the exercises that go with the Compass Pathways in the previous chapter before moving on to this chapter. You cannot really progress in any meaningful way unless you have a clear idea of what each of the eight compass pathways means for you. Without this sense of the eight compass pathways you are without a framework for your web. You need this framework so that you may place the helpers or teachers that you chose to weave in as you work.

In Chapter Two the idea of being able to weave your own web of life and also to weave in the connections or teachers, that you are drawn to working with, was introduced. It is now time to learn more about these connections or teachers, who they are and where they come from.

The connections that can become teachers for you represent the archetypal energies that you choose to work with as you move through your life. It is these teachers that can help bring you the insights and guidance that assist you in learning the lessons on your path. They come from you. In shamanic terms they bring powerful medicine to help you on your path.

An example of a teacher for many Peruvians who live by the Inca wheel is that of the Jaguar, which for them is a teacher of the West. This fits with their culture, their beliefs and their experience. However, when I was in the North of Peru I met a local man who told me that many Peruvians have Jaguar but in the North they have Fox because they do not know what a Jaguar is. In their culture Jaguar has no meaning but Fox does. This is an example of a teacher being chosen that fits those working with it.

In this way, as you continue, you too will be choosing

teachers that have meaning for you, that connect for you with one of the eight pathways in your web of life and in doing so you will be exploring what the teachers mean to you. As before, there are exercises that will help you to do this, but first you need a web.

Creating Your Web

Exercise 17

- Here you will find a blank web. The circles are spaces in which you can eventually write your teachers. There is room for forty teachers in this web. This may not sound like many but it is much easier to work initially if you do not make your web too big or have to cope with placing or working with too many energies.
- This web is yours to reproduce as many times as you need to for your own use.
- You can use this web or make one of your own if you would prefer.
- Decide which web you will use, the one here or your own and prepare it so you have it ready to work with later.

Blank Web of Life

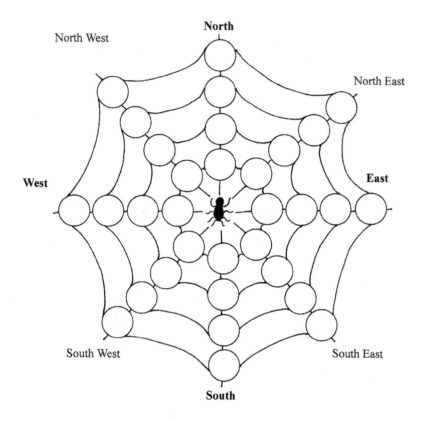

You can add teachers, enlarge your web and make any adjustments at any time in the future. This is your web and how you create it and what you weave into it is all part of your journey. It is right that it expands and grows as you do.

My own web has been through many adjustments. I have tried to fit in teachers that would not fit and which I eventually realized were not right for me. At one point I enlarged my web and then decided to leave space instead of filling it with extra teachers. I have also tried working with a smaller web and then felt hemmed in, so understood that for me, at this time, it was right to leave space. If there is no space then there is no room for anything new to come in. I am sure there will be many more adjustments in the future as I learn and develop, and so it will be for you but we all need to begin somewhere.

So, now that you have created or chosen a web as a framework in which to weave it is time to begin looking, finding the connections that for you may become teachers.

Finding Your Teachers

Remember it is important that the teachers you choose to weave into your web are teachers you feel drawn to working with. It is completely your choice as to whom you work with. For example, someone who works with or is drawn to angels, herbs or crystals may need to place more of these in their web. Indeed a crystal healer might have a web consisting only of crystals and stones for these may bring them all the teaching and guidance they need.

When you are choosing your teachers it is helpful to chose them in groups of four or eight as this allows you to weave them easily into your web, connecting them with one of the eight pathways as you do so.

Remember also that nothing is cast in stone. Teachers may come and teachers may go, you may need to add new ones in or replace some that you have been working with. This is ok. The way your web is woven, the teachers you choose to work with are yours and your web may be adapted at any time. So feel free to experiment, be creative, be adventurous, if something is not right for you it will be impossible for you to weave it into your web.

Exercise 18

- Take a large sheet of paper.
- Write down all the teachers you can think of whom you might like to work with.
- A good way to start is to think of what you already draw

into your life. Do you have a collection of anything? As a child, or even as an adult, is there a toy that is important to you? Are there plants you always have to have in your garden or home? Are their animals you are drawn to? Are you interested in or fascinated by anything in particular?

- If nothing comes to mind then create your sacred space, sit quietly within it and allow your mind to quieten and become still.
- In the stillness ask for your teachers to be shown to you.
- You may find words or images float into your mind or vision.
- If this happens wait until every thing that can come to you has come then slowly bring yourself back into the room and write down what you have received.
- Do not worry if nothing comes to you. It may mean that this was not a good time to be working so try again another time or try a different way.
- If you work with a pendulum you could use this to help you identify which teachers to work with.
- Look back at all the notes you have made whilst working with the compass pathways. There are sure to be teachers to be found in your notes.
- What you have is only a starting point. From now it is up to you to develop this. Just let your ideas flow.
- When you have a good list then divide it up into fours or eights if you have more than eight of anything e.g. ten animals, then select the eight that feel right at this time.

Ideas for your teachers

If you are completely stuck the following are some ideas for teachers. Make sure though that you only choose those teachers you feel really drawn to working with and which fit your beliefs and culture.

Although they are in loose groups this is only for ease of

reading, if you need to select from these teachers then group them in fours or eights in any way that feels right for you.

- Spring, summer, autumn, winter.
- Red, yellow, black, white, orange, violet, blue, green...
- Conception, birth, childhood, adolescence, maturity, old age, death.
- Earth, fire, air, water.
- Mind, physical body, spirit, emotions.
- Renewal, growth, insight, understanding.
- Wisdom, trust, illumination, creativity, healing, protection, inertia, unknown.
- Generosity, understanding, dreams, inner child, spontaneity, responsibility, love, self respect, fear, perseverance, anger, innocence, integrity, focus, honesty.
- Friends, colleagues and peers, family, partnerships...
- Imbolc, Vernal Equinox/Ostara Beltane, Summer Solstice/Litha, Lammas/Lughnassadh, Fall or Autumn Equinox/Mabon, Samhain, Winter Solstice/Yule.
- Mirth, reverence, honor, humility, strength, beauty, power, compassion.
- Sun, stars, planets, moon, other celestial beings, space, rainbow, clouds, sunrise, sunset, dusk, night.
- Thyme, fennel, dill, rosemary, anise, sage, garlic, basil, mint, parsley, coriander, angelica.
- Buffalo, wolf, snake or serpent, owl, snow goose, hummingbird, eagle, hawk, nightingale, lark, wren, sparrow, crow, robin, butterfly, dragonfly, bee, ladybird, beaver, deer, condor, mouse, salmon, rabbit, dog, whales, dolphins, sharks, otters, seals, walrus, starfish, crab, lobsters, seagull, duck, swan, heron, puffin, alligator, crocodile, frog, puma, jaguar, bear, raven, turtle, fox, moose, antelope, goat, sheep, squirrel, badger, monkey, pig.

- Animal kingdom, plant kingdom, mineral kingdom, human kingdom.
- Dancing, drumming, singing, playing, praying, meditating, seeing, thinking, being, listening.
- Cypress, oak, birch, willow, ash, hawthorn, cedar, redwood.
- Healers, ancestors, elders, guides, Spirit, Ascended Masters, Earth Goddess, Horned God.
- Inner child, inner warrior, inner sage, inner nurturer.
- Archangels Michael, Gabriel, Jophiel, Raphael.
- Rose, daffodil, tulip, lily, daisy, bluebell, foxglove, marigold.

These suggestions are by no means exhaustive but are simply starting points to help trigger your own teachers.

I am drawn to and know of many more teachers than I currently have in my own web but those I have woven in are enough for now. All of them feel right, all of them I connect to and all of them were reasonably easy to fit into the web and on the pathways.

When I was first weaving my own web, I desperately wanted to work with the Celtic festivals of Imbolc, Ostara, Beltane, Summer Solstice, Lammas, Mabon , Samhain, and Winter Solstice but no matter what I did I couldn't get them to fit into my web. On reflecting on what was happening I realized that I really only work with Summer and Winter Solstice and therefore I was trying to make teachers fit that really had no meaning for me at present and so could do nothing to help me. Once I had let go of the desire then other, more beneficial teachers were able to come in for me.

I also realized that in my own web I needed a lot of animals. This for me represents the shamanic elements of my work and thus all are very important to me. Each animal is there for a reason and their teachings and medicine bring me great understanding and support as well as lessons.

Have fun exploring and finding your own teachers, over time you will learn why they are there and the lessons they bring you even if it is not clear at the start.

Chapter Seven

Connecting With Your Teachers

Before you can weave your teachers into your web of life, begin to learn from them and use their energy to support and guide you, it is important to explore ways of connecting with them.

When you first learn to connect with the energy of something it can be easier to have whatever you are connecting with physically present. You may like to explore connecting with several different energies before you move on to work with your own teachers.

At this stage do not worry if you are not working with one of the teachers you have chosen for your web. This is more about gaining experience of connecting with other energies than connecting with your own teachers. Everything you do here will help you to form good connections with them when the time comes.

What follows are exercises you can try first of all with a tree or a plant. This is because when you begin it is easier to connect to something in nature that is living. You may then try and connect with as many different energies as you wish.

Exercise 19
- Choose a tree or plant to work with.
- Create sacred space wherever you have chosen to work.
- Move so that you are sitting close to the tree or plant.
- If possible you can pick the plant up and hold it or reach out and place your palm gently on the plant or tree.
- Check that you feel comfortable being with this teacher. If not then change your teacher.
- Sit quietly, breathe slowly and deeply so that you feel calm and relaxed.

- Ask the teacher you have chosen for permission to work with it.
- Ask if it will share its energy with you.
- Sit or stand quietly and breathe in the energy of the teacher.
- Feel its energy fill you, be aware of any sensations, emotions, images or words that come to you.
- Take your time with this but when you are ready write down everything that you experienced in your notebook.

Exercise 20

- Connect with the tree or plant in the same way as in Exercise 19.
- Sit or stand quietly and breathe in the energy of the teacher.
- Feel its energy fill you, be aware of any sensations, emotions, images or words that come to you.
- Ask the teacher if it has any teaching to share with you.
- Wait and see what comes to you. Listen not with your mind, but with the whole of your being.
- Take your time with this but when you are ready write down everything that came to you in your notebook.

Exercise 21

- Connect with the tree or plant in the same way as before.
- Sit or stand quietly and breathe in the energy of the teacher.
- Feel its energy fill you, be aware of any sensations, emotions, images or words that come to you.
- Ask to hear the song of the teacher you are working with.
- As before wait and see what comes to you. Listen not with your mind but with the whole of your being.
- Take your time with this but when you are ready write down everything that came to you in your notebook.

Exercise 22

- When you are happy connecting to plants and trees try connecting to crystals, stones, feathers i.e. teachers you can physically touch.
- Repeat Exercises 19 - 21 with your new teachers.

Exercise 23

- Instead of working with a teacher that is physically present write the name of one of your teachers on a piece of paper. This is because as you move on to work with your own teachers and weave them into your web it is unlikely that you will be able to make physical contact with all of those you choose to work with.
- Create sacred space wherever you have chosen to work.
- Hold the piece of paper with your teacher written on it between your hands.
  Sit quietly, breathe slowly and deeply so that you feel calm and relaxed.
- Ask your teacher to share its energy with you.
  Sit or stand quietly and breathe in the energy of the teacher.
- Feel its energy fill you, be aware of any sensations, emotions, images or words that come to you.
- Ask the teacher if it has any teaching or guidance to share with you.
- Ask to hear its song.
- Take your time with this and be prepared to repeat this step if needed.
- When you are ready write down everything that you experienced in your notebook.
- Repeat this exercise as many times as you wish to at this point.

The more you practice connecting with the energy of teachers the easier it will be for you to connect with your own teachers as you weave your web of life.

Take your time with these steps, practice and repeat them with different teachers until you feel comfortable connecting to different energies and receiving information from them.

Chapter Eight

Weaving In Your Teachers

Lady spin your circle bright
Weave your web of dark and light
Earth, air, fire and water
Bind us all as one
Ancient Pagan Chant

Hopefully by now you have a web to work in and teachers with which to work. If not you need to go back to the previous chapter and make sure you have both for now is the time to begin working with your teachers and finding out where they sit within your web.

When I first began weaving my own web of life I felt very strongly that the first teachers I needed to weave in were the elements. For me it is the elements that help to make the connections between everything both in my own web and beyond.

At first I only had vague thoughts of how to do this. I had ideas of spending a week holding the energy of each element, observing, meditating, journaling and in doing so, finding the direction which for me was the right one for each element. All of these ways would have been perfect ways of gaining understanding and information but in the end it was a shamanic journey that gave me the answers I was seeking.

I journeyed with the intention of finding which position the elements took for me. I saw a stream which suddenly stopped as if cut off and as I followed it I found it joined three other streams which also stopped suddenly in the same way. As I looked I saw they formed a cross. In the center was a golden fish swimming round and round in circles.

As I looked deeply into one of the streams I saw that the water in it was bubbling, another stream was full of blue shapes like glass, the third stream was full of steam and the fourth contained shoots of grass.

After puzzling over what I was seeing for a long time, I lay down, covered myself in my cloak and went to sleep both in ordinary and non-ordinary reality.

When eventually I awoke in ordinary reality I decided to re-enter the journey and so returned to non-ordinary reality where I stood up and made my way to the center where the four streams met. As I did so a fountain sprung up then died down. Testing the water I stepped into the center and with my hand opened up four more streams, one for each pathway or leg of the spider as I later realized.

As I stood there I realized I was being given the places where the elements belonged in my web of life and being shown where I needed to weave them in.

In the center was me the creator shown here first of all as the fish swimming round in circles which was exactly what I had been doing, then later as the fountain springing to life.

To the West is Earth represented by the green shoots.

To the North, Water shown to me as bubbling water.

To the East, Air, glass, like the sky.

And to the South, Fire represented here as steam.

These then became the four pathways into which I wove the elements and became the starting point for me.

My first teachers I therefore placed in their respective compass pathways North, East, South and West.

In the time since I have only ever come across one other person who connects the elements with the directions in the way that I do but that does not matter. This is my web, it belongs to me and is unique to me so whatever I place in it and wherever I place my teachers is also where they are right for me, and so it will be for you.

My second four teachers, the seasons, I then placed in North East, South East, North West, South West in the direction I felt they

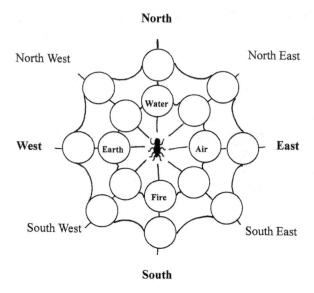

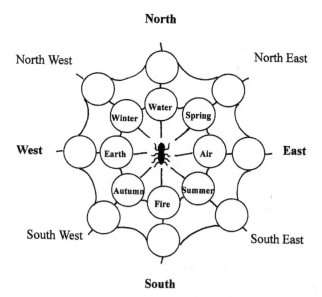

belonged in.

There are many ways in which you can find the positions in your web that your teachers are to be placed in. What is important is that you find a way to work that is useful for you. Much of weaving your web of life, is about exploring and experimenting so once again, don't be afraid to do this, the most profitable learning often comes in unexpected ways.

Exercise 24

You have already experimented with ways of connecting with your teachers and hopefully have found a way that works for you. You can now apply what you have learnt to see where your teachers need to be placed in your web.

You may find that you use a combination of ways including your own sense of knowing or intuition. What follows is a list of suggestions to remind you of some of the things you can try:

- Create your sacred space, sit quietly within it and allow your mind to quieten and become still.
- Play relaxing music, sit focusing on your teacher and see what information floats into your mind as to where this teacher needs to be for you. Trust whatever you are getting and write it down.
- Hold a piece of paper with the name of the teacher written on it. Meditate on the teacher asking for guidance on where to place it.
- Use your notebook to see if there is guidance there from when you were finding your teachers. You may well have the information you seek in your notes.
- If you know how to do shamanic journeys then try journeying.
- If you work with a pendulum use one to help you place your teachers.

In general

- The teachers that go in the center of the web in the first eight positions are those that you feel the closest to or work with most.

- Teachers are placed on the pathway that you feel corresponds to them best.
- If there are four teachers in a group place them on either North, South, East, West or North East, South East, North West, South West.
- If there are eight teachers in a group place them one in each pathway equidistant from the center.
- Start in the center and work outwards.

It's useful to write your teachers in pencil first, that way any adjustments or changes can be made without redoing the whole web. When you are happy with the placement of your teachers ink them in.

Example of a Completed Web of Life

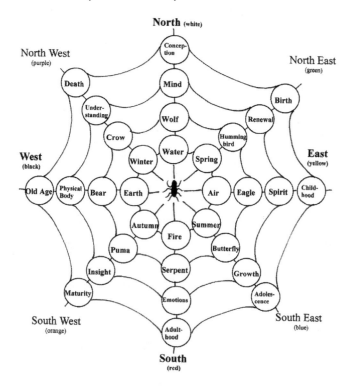

Chapter Nine

Creating Your Cards

To help you work with the teachers in your web you are going to make a card for each of your teachers and each of the compass pathways. This will eventually give you a pack of cards with which you may work.

It is very important that you make these cards for yourself and do not give them to someone else to do. The words and images that you put on the cards and the fact that **you** create them, builds **your** energy into the cards. This in turn helps to build the power of the cards thus making a stronger connection between you, the teacher and your web.

At every stage, just as you create your life, so you create the web, weave in the teachers you have chosen to work with and create the cards that will help you gain insight into the lessons they bring.

It does not matter how 'perfect' the cards are, whether you are the world's greatest artist, or not, whether you draw pictures, trace them or cut images that resonate, from magazines or books, what matters is that YOU create them.

Creating the cards will help you connect with the energy of the image you have drawn on the card and therefore the teacher itself. Creating the card helps you learn about the teacher as you work on creating the image. This will help you make a connection that, in the future, as you work with your web of life, will help you recognize the lessons you have chosen to receive.

The cards are yours; they will belong to you and are to be used by you and no one else. They will only be of relevance to you and so need only be seen by you. The cards only have value to you and not to anyone else.

What matters most is that the images on the cards make

sense to you. The images do not need to be the teachers themselves but something that for you represents the teacher.

For example, when I made my own cards I realized that I saw childhood as a bucket and spade, skipping rope and ball and saw adolescence as music. As I made my cards I also learnt about myself, the labels I put on things, the way I see things, so even as I made the cards the teachers were teaching me and so they will you.

Exercise 25

- You will need several sheets of card.
- Cut this card into 'playing card' size sections. Try to make them all the same size.
- You will need forty eight 'cards' in total although you might like to cut extra blanks as spares.
- You could also use business card blanks, as the cards are a suitable size for this.
- Decorate the backs of eight of these cards with something that represents to you the compass pathways e.g. a compass rose.
- Decorate the backs of the remaining cards with something that represents to you the web of life e.g. a spider's web.

Exercise 26

- You will need your notebook.
- As you make each card record what images or colors you are using on it and any insights you get into why you are using them.
- As you realize more about why you put certain images on cards record what you learn.
- Take note of any images that puzzle you and pay attention to any cards you struggle to find images for.
- The making of the cards and the insights you gain will teach you about yourself so take your time here.

When creating my own cards I wrote:

I have just realized that 'Emotions' I drew as tears but emotions are also laughter, happiness and joy. I realize that when I think of emotions I do always think of the negative aspects - sadness, confusion, anger, tantrums and tears.

This shows me that there is some work I need to do here and that the teacher of emotions is one that will be good for me to work with and to learn from.

Exercise 27

- For this you need eight Pathway Cards and all of your Web Card blanks.
- Sit with the cards and feel where to start. If it is with the Pathway Cards follow the Pathway Card task, or if you are starting with the Web Cards follow the Web Cards task.
- Do what feels right for you and whatever you are working on.
- Trust your instincts and intuition.

Pathway Cards

- On each of the Pathway Cards, write a direction. You might like to write this as words or as initials e.g. N, S, E, W, SE, SW, NE, NW.
- Decorate the cards with images that for you connect with the direction you are working with.
- You might also like to use a color that you connect with each particular direction.
- Be aware if there is theme that runs though the Pathway Cards. There may be or it may be that each card has something special but individual.

For me the theme of color ran through all my Pathway Cards but in addition there were two other themes. North, South, East and West had the theme of elements. For example my North card had a large N and an image of water representing the element. My N was then colored in white, being the color I connect with North. North East, South East, North West and South West though had their own theme of seasons.

Your theme, if you have one, will be different and will be something that resonates with you.

Web Cards

- Using the teachers you have chosen to work with begin making your Web Cards.
  In one corner write the initials of the direction you are placing your teacher in.
- Decorate the card with an image of your teacher.
- Continue until you have one Web Card for each of the teachers you have chosen.
- It is important to complete cards for all the teachers you have chosen to work with before you can begin working with your web.

Remember

With both the Pathway Cards and the Web Cards you can draw images, trace, use clip art, pictures cut from books or magazines etc but whatever you do make these cards yourself, do not ask anyone else to make them for you.

When completed, the sets of Pathway Cards and Web Cards are the sets you will work with.

When first making my own cards I drew all of the images on them in pencil and left them that way for a while. Having done this I realized that left in that state the cards lacked power and it was not until I had made the images permanent that I found they came to life. So do make sure you complete the cards and bring them to life.

You may have identified more teachers than you have chosen to weave into your web for now. This is useful as you can make additional cards for these teachers. Make them in the same way as you have your other Web Cards but do not give them a direction or place in your web. These cards can be used along with both Web Cards and Pathway Cards for daily guidance or additional insights and this will be looked at further in the next chapter.

Chapter Ten

Weaving Your Web of Life

A path that untangles the web
A path that brings home our power
Allowing each and every one of us
To become the spider
To learn to unravel and weave the
Web of life for ourselves
Runic John: (2010) Kindred Spirit Magazine

By now you have hopefully chosen your teachers, created your web and created your Pathway and Web Cards. It is now time to learn how to work with them and in doing so how to weave your own web of life.

There are many ways in which you will be able to work with your teachers and weave your web. What you will find here are only some possible ways of working. As you develop, explore and experiment you will find new ways, which are equal to, if not better, than the ones here, for they will be your own ways. As with everything else you have been doing, there is no right way and therefore no wrong way to work.

You can use your web of life to help you plan your path, either your path in life from this point onwards or your path connected with a project you are working on. Both of these are useful to do. You have a blank web to photocopy and use if you wish. There is no limit on the number of copies you may make so there is no end to the number or variety of paths you may weave.

So how can weaving a path through the web help you?

Most things in life have cycles, what we may perceive as being a beginning, middle and an end. In reality the whole of life is cyclical and so there are no true beginnings or endings but when one life event begins to move into another it can feel as if you are at the beginning of a cycle. Here, there is likely to be inspiration, excitement and new things happening, whereas if you are in the middle of something, it may be that there needs to be a period of stability or consolidation. Sometimes this can be misinterpreted as being on the wrong path or being stuck when in fact it may just be a misunderstanding of where you are. The perceived end of a path or cycle can also be difficult. Sometimes there may be things that need to be let go of before you can move on anew and move into a new phase, or there may be loose ends to be tied up. Again this can sometimes feel like a period where nothing is happening, or it may feel as if there is too much change. Whichever it is, knowing exactly where you are on your path and which teachers you are working with can help you decide what to do.

When you choose a path within your web you are simply choosing a way to walk and at the same time choosing some of the teachers who will work with you and help you on your path. By doing this you are creating your own life.

As with everything, as one path ends so another always begins. You will also find that there are paths within paths and cycles within cycles, for nothing happens in isolation. Each path or cycle may last a few hours, days, weeks, months or even years, according to how long it takes for you to learn what needs to be learnt or have the experiences that are there for you.

Weaving your path

There are several ways you can do this, as with everything else it is good to experiment and see what works for you. You may also find that you need different approaches at different times or when you have a different focus in mind.

Your Path

- You will need a blank web of life, your own completed web of life showing your teachers and your web cards.
- Hold the intention of what you may wish to weave a path for. This may be your life, or the path for a project you are working on.
- Sit quietly, focus on your breath and center yourself.
- Take your Web Cards, reaffirm your intention, shuffle the cards and draw one.
  You can do this by fanning out the cards face down and selecting one, or by shuffling the pack, cutting it and then taking the top card, or any other way that feels right for you.
  N.B. If a card falls out of your pack, then this is the card you use.
- The card you have chosen is your starting point. This gives you the place that you are in within your web of life, the direction you are working in and the teacher who is working with you.
- Take your completed web of life and check where this teacher is in your own web.
- Take the blank web and write in the teacher in the same position.
- Take your Web Cards again, shuffle them and choose a second card. This card is the teacher who will be at the end of this part of your path.
- Use your completed web of life to see where this teacher is in your own web and then fill this teacher in on the new web, on which you have just written the name of the teacher from the first card that you drew.
- You now have a new web showing the start and finish of the next part of your path.
- Using your intuition, working along the pathways, beginning at your starting point, draw a path that

connects these two teachers.

- You can move up or down pathways but can only move clockwise around your web, i.e. forwards.

- The longer the path you choose, the more teachers you will meet and the more you will learn.

- When you have chosen your path use your completed web of life, the one showing all your teachers, to fill in those you have chosen to work with for the next part of your life.

- This web will provide a record for you, so you know whom you have chosen to work with.

Example of Weaving a Life Path

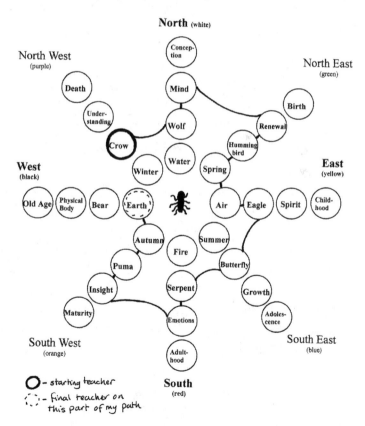

This web now shows the teachers for your path or those that will bring guidance or insight based on the intention you held at the start.

Sit with the first teacher on your path and see what they can share with you at this time. Be aware of who you are working with and look out for support, guidance and messages from them. Remember these may come through music, books, posters, overheard conversations, signs around you, insights or knowledge that comes to you, or any other way that your teachers can bring help in your direction.

The more you work with your teachers the more you will get a sense of when you have moved on to a new teacher. Trust your intuition.

Be aware also of the direction you are currently working in for there are lessons here for you as well. You might wish to remind yourself of the qualities that you generated for this direction in Chapter Five, Compass Pathways as each direction will bring its own energy and therefore its own medicine and lessons.

Identifying where you are on your path

Sometimes you will want to check where you are on your path. There are several ways you can do this.

Use your intuition

- Where do you feel you are based on the lessons you have been experiencing, the things you have been aware of and the observations you have made?
- The more you work with your teachers, the more you will get a sense of when you have moved on. Learn to trust your intuition.

Use your Pathway Cards

- Hold your intention, calm and center yourself.

- Shuffle your Pathway Cards and select one.
- This gives you the direction you are working in and therefore the pathway you are on.
- Check this pathway to see which teachers you have there and which teacher you feel you are working with.

Use your Web Cards

- If, having used your Pathway Cards you are still unsure of where you are because you have chosen more than one teacher on this pathway you can work with your Web Cards.
- Select the Web Cards for all the teachers you have currently chosen on this specific pathway.
  e.g. If I select the Pathway Card for North East then on my life path as shown in the **Example of Weaving a Life Path**, the Web Cards I would need to select are Spring, Hummingbird and Renewal.
- Shuffle your small selection of Web Cards and select one card.
- This is the teacher you are working with at present and the position you are in on your current life path.

Extending your path

- As your chosen life path comes towards the end you can extend your path by choosing the next part and the teachers you wish to connect and work with.
- You will need the web showing your current life path and your Web Cards.
- Hold the intention to plan the next part of your path.
- Sit quietly, focus on your breath and center yourself.
- Shuffle your Web Cards and select one.
- The final teacher on your current life path is the start of your new path and the card you have chosen is the final teacher of the next part of your path.

- Check your completed web of life to see where this teacher is and write their name on the web of life you are currently using.
- As you did when you planned the first part of your path use your intuition to connect these teachers. Remember you can go up and down pathways but only clockwise around your web, i.e. forwards.

Example of and Extended Life Path

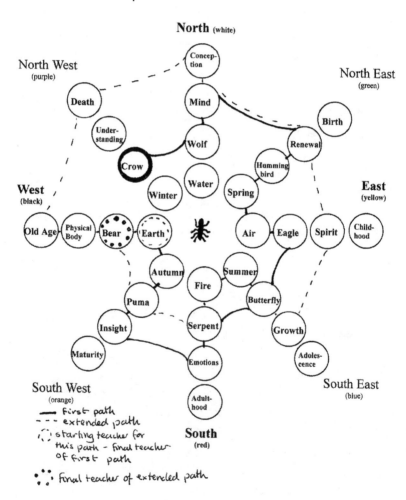

North (white)

North West
(purple)

North East
(green)

Death

Concep-
tion

Mind

Under-
standing

Birth

Wolf

Renewal

Crow

Humming
bird

West
(black)

Water

Winter

Spring

East
(yellow)

Old Age

Physical
Body

Bear

Earth

Air

Eagle

Spirit

Child-
hood

Autumn

Summer

Fire

Puma

Butterfly

Insight

Serpent

Growth

Maturity

Emotions

Adoles-
cence

South West
(orange)

South East
(blue)

Adult-
hood

—— first path
- - - extended path
⟨ ⟩ starting teacher for
this path - final teacher
of first path

South
(red)

∴ final teacher of extended path

You can meet teachers more than once as you move through your life paths. As you do so, because you have learnt previous lessons on your path you will have changed, developed and healed in some way. This means that you are now in a different place and the teachers you meet again will have new lessons or guidance for you.

You can extend your path as often as you wish either adding on to your last path or using a new blank web. Keep the web of life sheets for all the paths you weave, as this gives you a record of your journey, and shows the progress you are making. It also reminds you of the connections you have made within your web of life. By keeping the sheets you will always know where you have been, where you are and where you are going.

Choosing a teacher for general guidance

You can do this at any time just by shuffling your Web Cards and choosing a card from the pack. Sit with this teacher and see what guidance they bring.

You can also choose a Compass Card at any time to give you a sense of where you are. If you do this it is always good to look back and see what you connected with in that particular direction.

Choosing teachers for insight

Sometimes you just need to gain a little more insight into an area of your life and if so you can take a Pathway Card to see where you are and then the number of Web Cards that you feel will help you.

When I was writing this book I had planned both a life path and work path and had chosen teachers to help me, but in my writing I felt stuck and so needed some further insight.

The Pathway Card I chose was North East which was in fact the same direction I had started in on both my life path and work path. I had not moved from my starting direction at all.

This told me that there were lessons there I had not yet learnt and that I needed to still be there.

For me the North East connects with new beginnings, with spring and is a time where I know I need to be nurturing and patient. It is a time when I am in contact with the Eagle and with Spirit.

I chose four Web Cards, as this was the number that came to me and then sat with each teacher listening to what they had to tell me. All of the messages I received were clearly to do with my writing and advised me as to how to work.

Willow: For me Willow is a teacher that has no fixed position.

Be flexible; do not get too fixed in how and where writing is taking you. Be open to change as things grow and evolve.

Bear: For me Bear is a teacher of the West but it now comes to me in the North East.

Don't get carried away, remember there is still a need to be still, to look within and gain insight. Don't rush.

Rainbow: Rainbow is the second teacher with no fixed position emphasizing the need for me to be flexible perhaps.

Allow the light to shine on you as you work. Do not exclude anything; allow all aspects to feed the writing. Also connect to Spirit and your guides for guidance. Don't forget!

Water: For me Water is a teacher of the North but comes to me now in the North East.

Cleanse your thoughts as you work; allow the stagnant ones to be washed away leaving space for new ones to enter. Dynamic movement.

In my overall life plan, the teacher I was working with at this point was **Birth** and the teachers I had drawn for insight were helping me with the birth of my writing.

Using other card layouts

It is perfectly possible to work with any card layouts you know from working with other sets of cards as long as you have enough Web Cards to do so.

Lay the cards out as you would usually but instead of getting information from the words of others sit with your own teachers and let them work with you.

Your own way

As there is no right or wrong way of working with the cards and the web, you may in time find that you develop your own way, a way that makes complete sense for you. This is perfect. Take what you have here, use it, adapt it and make it completely your own. The only thing that is important is that it helps you, supports you and assists you in connecting with the teachers that are all around you everywhere.

Journaling

As you worked through the exercises 'the web of life' you have kept a notebook. If you have not already done so it would be a good idea to extend this so that it becomes a journal.

Keep a note of anything that feels significant, of the lessons that you are learning, of the signs, symbols, dreams and observations that come to you.

You can also journal the guidance that you receive as you sit with your teachers and connect with them. This way you will have opportunity to notice patterns and messages that you might otherwise overlook.

Along with the sheets showing the paths you have chosen to weave this will also help to give you a record of your journey through your web of life.

Where next?

Experiment.
Explore.
Learn.
Extend your web.
Make new connections by weaving in new teachers.

Grow.

Heal.

Have fun.

Whatever you do and wherever your path takes you, remember that you are the creator of that path, the spider weaving the web and making connections. You may not always like the lessons you are given but they are always the ones you need to help you, even if they do not feel like it at the time.

Remember that you always have a choice as to where you go, whom you work with and therefore the lessons you learn and the opportunities that cross your path.

Live your life to the full, knowing that you really are the one weaving your web of life.

References

Chapter One

1 A dams D *Dirk Gently's Holistic Detective Agency* (1988) U.K. Pan Books

2 Ingerman S (2011) *Shamanism: Healing of Individuals and the Planet* (abstract on shamanism) (online) Available from www.sandraingerman.com (Accessed 11 July 2012)

3 Eagle Soaring *The Interconnectedness of All ThingsTaught through Medicine Wheel Art* (online) Available from http://www.awarenessmag.com/julaug9/JA9_INTR.HTML (accessed 18th Jan 2011)

4 Lanza R with Berman B (April 2009) *Biocentrism: How Life and Consciousness Are the Keys to Understanding the True Nature of the Universe*: USA BenBella Books

5/6 Hamilton D R and Massey H (5 April 2012) *The Web of Life* (online) Available from http://www.healyourlife.com /author-harry-massey-and-david-r-hamilton-phd/2012/04/ wisdom/inspiration/the-web-of-life (Accessed 11 July 2012) Excerpted from(February 2012) *Choice Point: Align Your Purpose* UK Hay House

Chapter 10

John R. (Jan/Feb 2010) U.K. Kindred Spirit Magazine Issue 102

Moon Books invites you to begin or deepen your encounter with Paganism, in all its rich, creative, flourishing forms.